This Journal
Belongs to

_____

Date: ___ ___ Mon Tue Wed Thu Fri Sat Sun

Morning Routine

Today's positive affirmation:

Today's intention:

What I can control:

What I can't control:

Mindfulness exercises:
1.

2.

3.

4.

Evening Routine

Best thing about today: _____

_____

I'm grateful for:

Brain dump:

_____

_____

_____

_____

_____

_____

Self-care:

1. _____ ☐

2. _____ ☐

3. _____ ☐

4. _____ ☐

5. _____ ☐

Date: ___ ___ Mon Tue Wed Thu Fri Sat Sun

Morning Routine

Today's positive affirmation:

Today's intention: _____

What I can control:

What I can't control:

Mindfulness exercises:
1.
2.
3.
4.

Evening Routine

Best thing about today: _____

_____

I'm grateful for:

Brain dump:

_____

_____

_____

_____

_____

_____

_____

Self-care:

1. _____ ☐

2. _____ ☐

3. _____ ☐

4. _____ ☐

5. _____ ☐

Date: ___ ___ Mon Tue Wed Thu Fri Sat Sun

Morning Routine

Today's positive affirmation:

Today's intention:

What I can control:

What I can't control:

Mindfulness exercises:
1.
2.
3.
4.

Evening Routine

Best thing about today: _____

_____

I'm grateful for:

Brain dump:

_____

_____

_____

_____

_____

_____

Self-care:

1. _____ ☐

2. _____ ☐

3. _____ ☐

4. _____ ☐

5. _____ ☐

Date: ___ ___ Mon Tue Wed Thu Fri Sat Sun

Morning Routine

Today's positive affirmation:

Today's intention: _____

What I can control:

What I can't control:

Mindfulness exercises:
1.
2.
3.
4.

Evening Routine

Best thing about today: _____

_____

I'm grateful for:

Brain dump:

_____

_____

_____

_____

_____

_____

Self-care:

1. _____ ☐

2. _____ ☐

3. _____ ☐

4. _____ ☐

5. _____ ☐

Date: ___ ___ Mon Tue Wed Thu Fri Sat Sun

Morning Routine

Today's positive affirmation:

Today's intention: _____

_____

_____

What I can control:

What I can't control:

Mindfulness exercises:
1.
_____
2.
_____
3.
_____
4.
_____

Evening Routine

Best thing about today: _____

_____

I'm grateful for:

Brain dump:

_____

_____

_____

_____

_____

_____

_____

Self-care:

1. _____ ☐

2. _____ ☐

3. _____ ☐

4. _____ ☐

5. _____ ☐

Date: ___ ___ Mon Tue Wed Thu Fri Sat Sun

Morning Routine

Today's positive affirmation:

Today's intention:

What I can control:

What I can't control:

Mindfulness exercises:
1.
2.
3.
4.

Evening Routine

Best thing about today: _____

_____

I'm grateful for:

Brain dump:

_____

_____

_____

_____

_____

_____

_____

Self-care:

1. _____ ☐
2. _____ ☐
3. _____ ☐
4. _____ ☐
5. _____ ☐

Date: ___ ___ Mon Tue Wed Thu Fri Sat Sun

Morning Routine

Today's positive affirmation:

Today's intention:

What I can control:

What I can't control:

Mindfulness exercises:
1.
2.
3.
4.

Evening Routine

Best thing about today: _____

_____

I'm grateful for:

Brain dump:

_____

_____

_____

_____

_____

_____

_____

Self-care:

1.	☐
2.	☐
3.	☐
4.	☐
5.	☐

Date: ___ ___   Mon   Tue   Wed   Thu   Fri   Sat   Sun

Morning Routine

Today's positive affirmation:

Today's intention: _____

What I can control:

What I can't control:

Mindfulness exercises:

1.

2.

3.

4.

Evening Routine

Best thing about today: _____

_____

I'm grateful for:

Brain dump:

_____
_____
_____
_____
_____
_____
_____

Self-care:

1. _____ ☐
2. _____ ☐
3. _____ ☐
4. _____ ☐
5. _____ ☐

Date: ___ ___ Mon Tue Wed Thu Fri Sat Sun

Morning Routine

Today's positive affirmation:

Today's intention: _____

_____

_____

What I can control:

What I can't control:

Mindfulness exercises:
1. _____
2. _____
3. _____
4. _____

Evening Routine

Best thing about today: _____

_____

I'm grateful for:

Brain dump:

Self-care:

1. ☐
2. ☐
3. ☐
4. ☐
5. ☐

Date: ___ ___ Mon Tue Wed Thu Fri Sat Sun

Morning Routine

Today's positive affirmation:

Today's intention:

What I can control:

What I can't control:

Mindfulness exercises:

1.

2.

3.

4.

Evening Routine

Best thing about today: _____

_____

I'm grateful for:

Brain dump:

_____

_____

_____

_____

_____

_____

Self-care:

1. _____ ☐

2. _____ ☐

3. _____ ☐

4. _____ ☐

5. _____ ☐

Date: ___ ___ Mon Tue Wed Thu Fri Sat Sun

Morning Routine

Today's positive affirmation:

Today's intention:

What I can control:

What I can't control:

Mindfulness exercises:

1.

2.

3.

4.

Evening Routine

Best thing about today: _____

_____

I'm grateful for:

Brain dump:

_____

_____

_____

_____

_____

_____

_____

Self-care:

1. ☐

2. ☐

3. ☐

4. ☐

5. ☐

Date: ___ ___ Mon Tue Wed Thu Fri Sat Sun

Morning Routine

Today's positive affirmation:

Today's intention:

What I can control:

What I can't control:

Mindfulness exercises:
1.

2.

3.

4.

Evening Routine

Best thing about today: _____

_____

I'm grateful for:

Brain dump:

_____

_____

_____

_____

_____

_____

_____

Self-care:

1. _____ ☐

2. _____ ☐

3. _____ ☐

4. _____ ☐

5. _____ ☐

Date: ___ ___ Mon Tue Wed Thu Fri Sat Sun

Morning Routine

Today's positive affirmation:

Today's intention: _____

What I can control:

What I can't control:

Mindfulness exercises:

1.

2.

3.

4.

Evening Routine

Best thing about today: _____

_____

I'm grateful for:

Brain dump:

Self-care:

1. ☐
2. ☐
3. ☐
4. ☐
5. ☐

Date: ___ ___ Mon Tue Wed Thu Fri Sat Sun

Morning Routine

Today's positive affirmation:

Today's intention:

What I can control:

What I can't control:

Mindfulness exercises:

1.

2.

3.

4.

Evening Routine

Best thing about today: _____

_____

I'm grateful for:

Brain dump:

_____

_____

_____

_____

_____

_____

_____

Self-care:

1. _____ ☐

2. _____ ☐

3. _____ ☐

4. _____ ☐

5. _____ ☐

Date: ___ ___ Mon Tue Wed Thu Fri Sat Sun

Morning Routine

Today's positive affirmation:

Today's intention:

What I can control:

What I can't control:

Mindfulness exercises:

1.

2.

3.

4.

Evening Routine

Best thing about today: _____

_____

I'm grateful for:

Brain dump:

_____

_____

_____

_____

_____

_____

_____

Self-care:

1.	☐
2.	☐
3.	☐
4.	☐
5.	☐

Date: ___ ___ Mon Tue Wed Thu Fri Sat Sun

Morning Routine

Today's positive affirmation:

Today's intention:

What I can control:

What I can't control:

Mindfulness exercises:

1.

2.

3.

4.

Evening Routine

Best thing about today: _____

_____

I'm grateful for:

Brain dump:

_____

_____

_____

_____

_____

_____

_____

Self-care:

1. ☐

2. ☐

3. ☐

4. ☐

5. ☐

Date: ___ ___ Mon Tue Wed Thu Fri Sat Sun

Morning Routine

Today's positive affirmation:

Today's intention:

What I can control:

What I can't control:

Mindfulness exercises:
1.
2.
3.
4.

Evening Routine

Best thing about today: _____

_____

I'm grateful for:

Brain dump:

_____

_____

_____

_____

_____

_____

_____

Self-care:

1. _____ ☐

2. _____ ☐

3. _____ ☐

4. _____ ☐

5. _____ ☐

Date: _____ _____ Mon Tue Wed Thu Fri Sat Sun

Morning Routine

Today's positive affirmation:

Today's intention: _____

_____

_____

What I can control:

What I can't control:

Mindfulness exercises:
1. _____
2. _____
3. _____
4. _____

Evening Routine

Best thing about today: _____

_____

I'm grateful for:

Brain dump:

_____

_____

_____

_____

_____

_____

_____

Self-care:

1. _____ ☐

2. _____ ☐

3. _____ ☐

4. _____ ☐

5. _____ ☐

Date: ___ ___ Mon Tue Wed Thu Fri Sat Sun

Morning Routine

Today's positive affirmation:

Today's intention:

What I can control:

What I can't control:

Mindfulness exercises:

1.

2.

3.

4.

Evening Routine

Best thing about today: _____

_____

I'm grateful for:

Brain dump:

_____

_____

_____

_____

_____

_____

_____

Self-care:

1.	☐
2.	☐
3.	☐
4.	☐
5.	☐

Date: ___ ___ Mon Tue Wed Thu Fri Sat Sun

Morning Routine

Today's positive affirmation:

Today's intention: _____

_____

_____

What I can control:

What I can't control:

Mindfulness exercises:
1.
2.
3.
4.

Evening Routine

Best thing about today: _____

_____

I'm grateful for:

Brain dump:

_____

_____

_____

_____

_____

_____

_____

Self-care:

1. _____ ☐

2. _____ ☐

3. _____ ☐

4. _____ ☐

5. _____ ☐

Date: ___ ___ Mon Tue Wed Thu Fri Sat Sun

Morning Routine

Today's positive affirmation:

Today's intention:

What I can control:

What I can't control:

Mindfulness exercises:

1.

2.

3.

4.

Evening Routine

Best thing about today: _____

_____

I'm grateful for:

Brain dump:

_____

_____

_____

_____

_____

_____

Self-care:

1. _____ ☐

2. _____ ☐

3. _____ ☐

4. _____ ☐

5. _____ ☐

Date: ___ ___ Mon Tue Wed Thu Fri Sat Sun

Morning Routine

Today's positive affirmation:

Today's intention: ___

What I can control:

What I can't control:

Mindfulness exercises:
1.
2.
3.
4.

Evening Routine

Best thing about today: _____

_____

I'm grateful for:

Brain dump:

_____
_____
_____
_____
_____
_____
_____

Self-care:

1. _____ ☐
2. _____ ☐
3. _____ ☐
4. _____ ☐
5. _____ ☐

Date: ___ ___ Mon Tue Wed Thu Fri Sat Sun

Morning Routine

Today's positive affirmation:

Today's intention:

What I can control:

What I can't control:

Mindfulness exercises:

1.

2.

3.

4.

Evening Routine

Best thing about today: _____

_____

I'm grateful for:

Brain dump:

_____

_____

_____

_____

_____

_____

_____

Self-care:

1.	☐
2.	☐
3.	☐
4.	☐
5.	☐

Date: ___ ___ Mon Tue Wed Thu Fri Sat Sun

Morning Routine

Today's positive affirmation:

Today's intention:

What I can control:

What I can't control:

Mindfulness exercises:
1.
2.
3.
4.

Evening Routine

Best thing about today: _____

_____

I'm grateful for:

Brain dump:

_____

_____

_____

_____

_____

_____

_____

Self-care:

1. _____ ☐

2. _____ ☐

3. _____ ☐

4. _____ ☐

5. _____ ☐

Date: ___ ___ Mon Tue Wed Thu Fri Sat Sun

Morning Routine

Today's positive affirmation:

Today's intention:

What I can control:

What I can't control:

Mindfulness exercises:

1.

2.

3.

4.

Evening Routine

Best thing about today: _____

_____

I'm grateful for:

Brain dump:

_____

_____

_____

_____

_____

_____

_____

Self-care:

1.		☐
2.		☐
3.		☐
4.		☐
5.		☐

Date: ___ ___   Mon Tue Wed Thu Fri Sat Sun

Morning Routine

Today's positive affirmation:

Today's intention: _____

_____

_____

What I can control:

What I can't control:

Mindfulness exercises:

1. _____

2. _____

3. _____

4. _____

Evening Routine

Best thing about today: _____

_____

I'm grateful for:

Brain dump:
_____
_____
_____
_____
_____
_____
_____

Self-care:

1. _____ ☐

2. _____ ☐

3. _____ ☐

4. _____ ☐

5. _____ ☐

Date: ___ ___ Mon Tue Wed Thu Fri Sat Sun

Morning Routine

Today's positive affirmation:

Today's intention: _____

What I can control:

What I can't control:

Mindfulness exercises:

1. _____

2. _____

3. _____

4. _____

Evening Routine

Best thing about today: _____

_____

I'm grateful for:

Brain dump:

_____

_____

_____

_____

_____

_____

_____

Self-care:

1.	☐
2.	☐
3.	☐
4.	☐
5.	☐

Date: ___ ___ Mon Tue Wed Thu Fri Sat Sun

Morning Routine

Today's positive affirmation:

Today's intention:

What I can control:

What I can't control:

Mindfulness exercises:
1.

2.

3.

4.

Evening Routine

Best thing about today: _____

_____

I'm grateful for:

Brain dump:

_____

_____

_____

_____

_____

_____

_____

Self-care:

1. _____ ☐

2. _____ ☐

3. _____ ☐

4. _____ ☐

5. _____ ☐

Date: ___ ___ Mon Tue Wed Thu Fri Sat Sun

Morning Routine

Today's positive affirmation:

Today's intention: _____

What I can control:

What I can't control:

Mindfulness exercises:

1. _____

2. _____

3. _____

4. _____

Evening Routine

Best thing about today: _____

_____

I'm grateful for:

Brain dump:

_____

_____

_____

_____

_____

_____

_____

Self-care:

1. ☐

2. ☐

3. ☐

4. ☐

5. ☐

Date: ___ ___ Mon Tue Wed Thu Fri Sat Sun

Morning Routine

Today's positive affirmation:

Today's intention:

What I can control:

What I can't control:

Mindfulness exercises:
1.

2.

3.

4.

Evening Routine

Best thing about today: _____

_____

I'm grateful for:

Brain dump:

_____

_____

_____

_____

_____

_____

_____

Self-care:

1.	☐
2.	☐
3.	☐
4.	☐
5.	☐

Date: ___ ___ Mon Tue Wed Thu Fri Sat Sun

Morning Routine

Today's positive affirmation:

Today's intention:

What I can control:

What I can't control:

Mindfulness exercises:

1.

2.

3.

4.

Evening Routine

Best thing about today: _____

_____

I'm grateful for:

Brain dump:

_____

_____

_____

_____

_____

_____

_____

Self-care:

1.	☐
2.	☐
3.	☐
4.	☐
5.	☐

Date: ___ ___   Mon Tue Wed Thu Fri Sat Sun

Morning Routine

Today's positive affirmation:

Today's intention: _____

What I can control:

What I can't control:

Mindfulness exercises:

1.

2.

3.

4.

Evening Routine

Best thing about today: _____

_____

I'm grateful for:

Brain dump:

_____

_____

_____

_____

_____

_____

_____

Self-care:

1. _____ ☐

2. _____ ☐

3. _____ ☐

4. _____ ☐

5. _____ ☐

Date: ___ ___ Mon Tue Wed Thu Fri Sat Sun

Morning Routine

Today's positive affirmation:

Today's intention:

What I can control:

What I can't control:

Mindfulness exercises:

1.

2.

3.

4.

Evening Routine

Best thing about today: _____

_____

I'm grateful for:

Brain dump:

_____

_____

_____

_____

_____

_____

_____

Self-care:

1. _____ ☐

2. _____ ☐

3. _____ ☐

4. _____ ☐

5. _____ ☐

Date: ___ ___ Mon Tue Wed Thu Fri Sat Sun

Morning Routine

Today's positive affirmation:

Today's intention:

What I can control:

What I can't control:

Mindfulness exercises:
1.

2.

3.

4.

Evening Routine

Best thing about today: _____

_____

I'm grateful for:

Brain dump:

_____

_____

_____

_____

_____

_____

_____

Self-care:

1. _____ ☐

2. _____ ☐

3. _____ ☐

4. _____ ☐

5. _____ ☐

Date: ___ ___ Mon Tue Wed Thu Fri Sat Sun

Morning Routine

Today's positive affirmation:

Today's intention: _____

_____

_____

What I can control:

What I can't control:

Mindfulness exercises:
1.

2.

3.

4.

Evening Routine

Best thing about today: _____

_____

I'm grateful for:

Brain dump:

_____

_____

_____

_____

_____

_____

Self-care:

1. _____ ☐

2. _____ ☐

3. _____ ☐

4. _____ ☐

5. _____ ☐

Date: ___ ___ Mon Tue Wed Thu Fri Sat Sun

Morning Routine

Today's positive affirmation:

Today's intention:

What I can control:

What I can't control:

Mindfulness exercises:
1.

2.

3.

4.

Evening Routine

Best thing about today: _____

_____

I'm grateful for:

Brain dump:

_____

_____

_____

_____

_____

_____

Self-care:

1. _____ ☐

2. _____ ☐

3. _____ ☐

4. _____ ☐

5. _____ ☐

Date: ___ ___ Mon Tue Wed Thu Fri Sat Sun

Morning Routine

Today's positive affirmation:

Today's intention: _____

What I can control:

What I can't control:

Mindfulness exercises:
1.

2.

3.

4.

Evening Routine

Best thing about today:

_____

I'm grateful for:

Brain dump:

Self-care:

1.

2.

3.

4.

5.

Date: ___ ___ Mon Tue Wed Thu Fri Sat Sun

Morning Routine

Today's positive affirmation:

Today's intention:

What I can control:

What I can't control:

Mindfulness exercises:

1.

2.

3.

4.

Evening Routine

est thing about today: _____

_____

'm grateful for:

rain dump:

_____

_____

_____

_____

_____

_____

elf-care:

1.	☐
2.	☐
3.	☐
4.	☐
5.	☐

Date: ___ ___ Mon Tue Wed Thu Fri Sat Sun

Morning Routine

Today's positive affirmation:

Today's intention:

What I can control:

What I can't control:

Mindfulness exercises:
1.

2.

3.

4.

Evening Routine

Best thing about today:

_____

I'm grateful for:

Brain dump:

Self-care:

1. ☐
2. ☐
3. ☐
4. ☐
5. ☐

Date: ___ ___ Mon Tue Wed Thu Fri Sat Sun

Morning Routine

Today's positive affirmation:

Today's intention:

What I can control:

What I can't control:

Mindfulness exercises:
1.
2.
3.
4.

Evening Routine

Best thing about today: _____

_____

I'm grateful for:

Brain dump:

_____

_____

_____

_____

_____

_____

_____

Self-care:

1. _____ ☐

2. _____ ☐

3. _____ ☐

4. _____ ☐

5. _____ ☐

Date: ___ ___ Mon Tue Wed Thu Fri Sat Sun

Morning Routine

Today's positive affirmation:

Today's intention:

What I can control:

What I can't control:

Mindfulness exercises:
1.
2.
3.
4.

Evening Routine

Best thing about today: _____

_____

I'm grateful for:

Brain dump:

_____

_____

_____

_____

_____

_____

_____

Self-care:

1. _____ ☐

2. _____ ☐

3. _____ ☐

4. _____ ☐

5. _____ ☐

Date: ___ ___ Mon Tue Wed Thu Fri Sat Sun

Morning Routine

Today's positive affirmation:

Today's intention:

What I can control:

What I can't control:

Mindfulness exercises:
1.
2.
3.
4.

Evening Routine

Best thing about today: _____

_____

I'm grateful for:

Brain dump:

_____

_____

_____

_____

_____

_____

_____

Self-care:

1. _____ ☐

2. _____ ☐

3. _____ ☐

4. _____ ☐

5. _____ ☐

Date: ____ ____ Mon Tue Wed Thu Fri Sat Sun

Morning Routine

Today's positive affirmation:

Today's intention:

What I can control:

What I can't control:

Mindfulness exercises:

1.

2.

3.

4.

Evening Routine

Best thing about today: _____

_____

I'm grateful for:

Brain dump:

_____

_____

_____

_____

_____

_____

_____

Self-care:

1. _____ ☐

2. _____ ☐

3. _____ ☐

4. _____ ☐

5. _____ ☐

Date: ___ ___ Mon Tue Wed Thu Fri Sat Sun

Morning Routine

Today's positive affirmation:

Today's intention: _____

_____

_____

What I can control:

What I can't control:

Mindfulness exercises:

1. _____

2. _____

3. _____

4. _____

Evening Routine

Best thing about today: _____

_____

I'm grateful for:

Brain dump:

_____

_____

_____

_____

_____

_____

Self-care:

1. _____ ☐

2. _____ ☐

3. _____ ☐

4. _____ ☐

5. _____ ☐

Date: ___ ___ Mon Tue Wed Thu Fri Sat Sun

Morning Routine

Today's positive affirmation:

Today's intention:

What I can control:

What I can't control:

Mindfulness exercises:
1.
2.
3.
4.

Evening Routine

Best thing about today: _____

_____

I'm grateful for:

Brain dump:

_____

_____

_____

_____

_____

_____

_____

Self-care:

1. _____ ☐

2. _____ ☐

3. _____ ☐

4. _____ ☐

5. _____ ☐

Date: ___ ___ Mon Tue Wed Thu Fri Sat Sun

Morning Routine

Today's positive affirmation:

Today's intention:

What I can control:

What I can't control:

Mindfulness exercises:

1.

2.

3.

4.

Evening Routine

Best thing about today: _____

_____

I'm grateful for:

Brain dump:

_____

_____

_____

_____

_____

_____

_____

Self-care:

1.	☐
2.	☐
3.	☐
4.	☐
5.	☐

Date: ___ ___ Mon Tue Wed Thu Fri Sat Sun

Morning Routine

Today's positive affirmation:

Today's intention: _____

What I can control:

What I can't control:

Mindfulness exercises:
1.
2.
3.
4.

Evening Routine

Best thing about today: _____

_____

I'm grateful for:

Brain dump:

_____

_____

_____

_____

_____

_____

_____

Self-care:

1. _____ ☐

2. _____ ☐

3. _____ ☐

4. _____ ☐

5. _____ ☐

Date: ____ ____ Mon Tue Wed Thu Fri Sat Sun

Morning Routine

Today's positive affirmation:

Today's intention: _____

What I can control:

What I can't control:

Mindfulness exercises:
1.
2.
3.
4.

Evening Routine

Best thing about today: _____

_____

I'm grateful for:

Brain dump:

_____

_____

_____

_____

_____

_____

_____

Self-care:

1. _____ ☐

2. _____ ☐

3. _____ ☐

4. _____ ☐

5. _____ ☐

Date: ____ ____ Mon Tue Wed Thu Fri Sat Sun

Morning Routine

Today's positive affirmation:

Today's intention:

What I can control:

What I can't control:

Mindfulness exercises:

1.

2.

3.

4.

Evening Routine

Best thing about today: _____

_____

I'm grateful for:

Brain dump:

_____

_____

_____

_____

_____

_____

Self-care:

1. _____ ☐

2. _____ ☐

3. _____ ☐

4. _____ ☐

5. _____ ☐

Date: ___ ___ Mon Tue Wed Thu Fri Sat Sun

Morning Routine

Today's positive affirmation:

Today's intention:

What I can control:

What I can't control:

Mindfulness exercises:

1.

2.

3.

4.

Evening Routine

Best thing about today: _____

_____

I'm grateful for:

Brain dump:

_____

_____

_____

_____

_____

_____

_____

Self-care:

1. _____ ☐

2. _____ ☐

3. _____ ☐

4. _____ ☐

5. _____ ☐

Date: ___ ___ Mon Tue Wed Thu Fri Sat Sun

Morning Routine

Today's positive affirmation:

Today's intention:

What I can control:

What I can't control:

Mindfulness exercises:
1.
2.
3.
4.

Evening Routine

Best thing about today: _____

_____

I'm grateful for:

Brain dump:

_____
_____
_____
_____
_____
_____
_____

Self-care:

1. _____ ☐

2. _____ ☐

3. _____ ☐

4. _____ ☐

5. _____ ☐

Date: ___ ___ Mon Tue Wed Thu Fri Sat Sun

Morning Routine

Today's positive affirmation:

Today's intention:

What I can control:

What I can't control:

Mindfulness exercises:

1.

2.

3.

4.

Evening Routine

Best thing about today:

_____

_____

I'm grateful for:

Brain dump:

_____

_____

_____

_____

_____

_____

_____

Self-care:

1. _____ ☐

2. _____ ☐

3. _____ ☐

4. _____ ☐

5. _____ ☐

Date: ___ ___ Mon Tue Wed Thu Fri Sat Sun

Morning Routine

Today's positive affirmation:

Today's intention:

What I can control:

What I can't control:

Mindfulness exercises:
1.

2.

3.

4.

Evening Routine

Best thing about today: _____

_____

I'm grateful for:

Brain dump:

_____

_____

_____

_____

_____

_____

_____

Self-care:

1. _____ ☐

2. _____ ☐

3. _____ ☐

4. _____ ☐

5. _____ ☐

Date: ___ ___ Mon Tue Wed Thu Fri Sat Sun

Morning Routine

Today's positive affirmation:

Today's intention: _____

_____

_____

What I can control:

What I can't control:

Mindfulness exercises:

1.

2.

3.

4.

Evening Routine

Best thing about today: _____

_____

I'm grateful for:

Brain dump:

_____

_____

_____

_____

_____

_____

Self-care:

1. _____ ☐

2. _____ ☐

3. _____ ☐

4. _____ ☐

5. _____ ☐

Date: ___ ___ Mon Tue Wed Thu Fri Sat Sun

Morning Routine

Today's positive affirmation:

Today's intention:

What I can control:

What I can't control:

Mindfulness exercises:
1.
2.
3.
4.

Evening Routine

Best thing about today: _____

_____

I'm grateful for:

Brain dump:

_____

_____

_____

_____

_____

_____

_____

Self-care:

1. _____ ☐

2. _____ ☐

3. _____ ☐

4. _____ ☐

5. _____ ☐

Date: ___ ___ Mon Tue Wed Thu Fri Sat Sun

Morning Routine

Today's positive affirmation:

Today's intention:

What I can control:

What I can't control:

Mindfulness exercises:

1.

2.

3.

4.

Evening Routine

Best thing about today: _____

_____

I'm grateful for:

Brain dump:

_____

_____

_____

_____

_____

_____

Self-care:

1. _____ ☐

2. _____ ☐

3. _____ ☐

4. _____ ☐

5. _____ ☐

Date: ___ ___ Mon Tue Wed Thu Fri Sat Sun

Morning Routine

Today's positive affirmation:

Today's intention:

What I can control:

What I can't control:

Mindfulness exercises:

1.

2.

3.

4.

Evening Routine

Best thing about today: _____

_____

I'm grateful for:

Brain dump:

_____

_____

_____

_____

_____

_____

Self-care:

1. _____ ☐

2. _____ ☐

3. _____ ☐

4. _____ ☐

5. _____ ☐

Date: ___ ___ Mon Tue Wed Thu Fri Sat Sun

Morning Routine

Today's positive affirmation:

Today's intention:

What I can control:

What I can't control:

Mindfulness exercises:
1.
2.
3.
4.

Evening Routine

Best thing about today: _____

_____

I'm grateful for:

Brain dump:

_____

_____

_____

_____

_____

_____

_____

Self-care:

1. _____ ☐

2. _____ ☐

3. _____ ☐

4. _____ ☐

5. _____ ☐

Date: ___ ___ Mon Tue Wed Thu Fri Sat Sun

Morning Routine

Today's positive affirmation:

Today's intention:

What I can control:

What I can't control:

Mindfulness exercises:

1.

2.

3.

4.

Evening Routine

Best thing about today:

_____

_____

I'm grateful for:

Brain dump:

_____

_____

_____

_____

_____

_____

Self-care:

1.	☐
2.	☐
3.	☐
4.	☐
5.	☐

Made in United States
North Haven, CT
13 March 2022

17062903R00074